Lisa Weir

Contents

Birthdays

How do you like to **celebrate** your birthday?

Do you have a cake with candles?

Do you have a party with family and friends?

Around the world, children celebrate their birthdays in different ways.

A Birthday Cake

In Indonesia, some children have a birthday cake made of rice.

The rice is made into a cone shape. Vegetables and meat are placed around the cone.

A Birthday Wreath

In Germany, some children have a special **wreath** for their birthday candles.

The wreath is made from wood.
It holds candles that burn all day.

A Birthday Drink

In Sudan, some children have a special drink on their birthday.

The drink is made from **hibiscus** (say *hy-biss-kus*) flowers. It is red and it tastes sweet.

A Birthday Game

In Australia, some children play games on their birthday.

One game is called pass-the-**parcel**. Children sit in a circle and take turns to unwrap the parcel.

The last child to unwrap the parcel gets to keep the present inside.

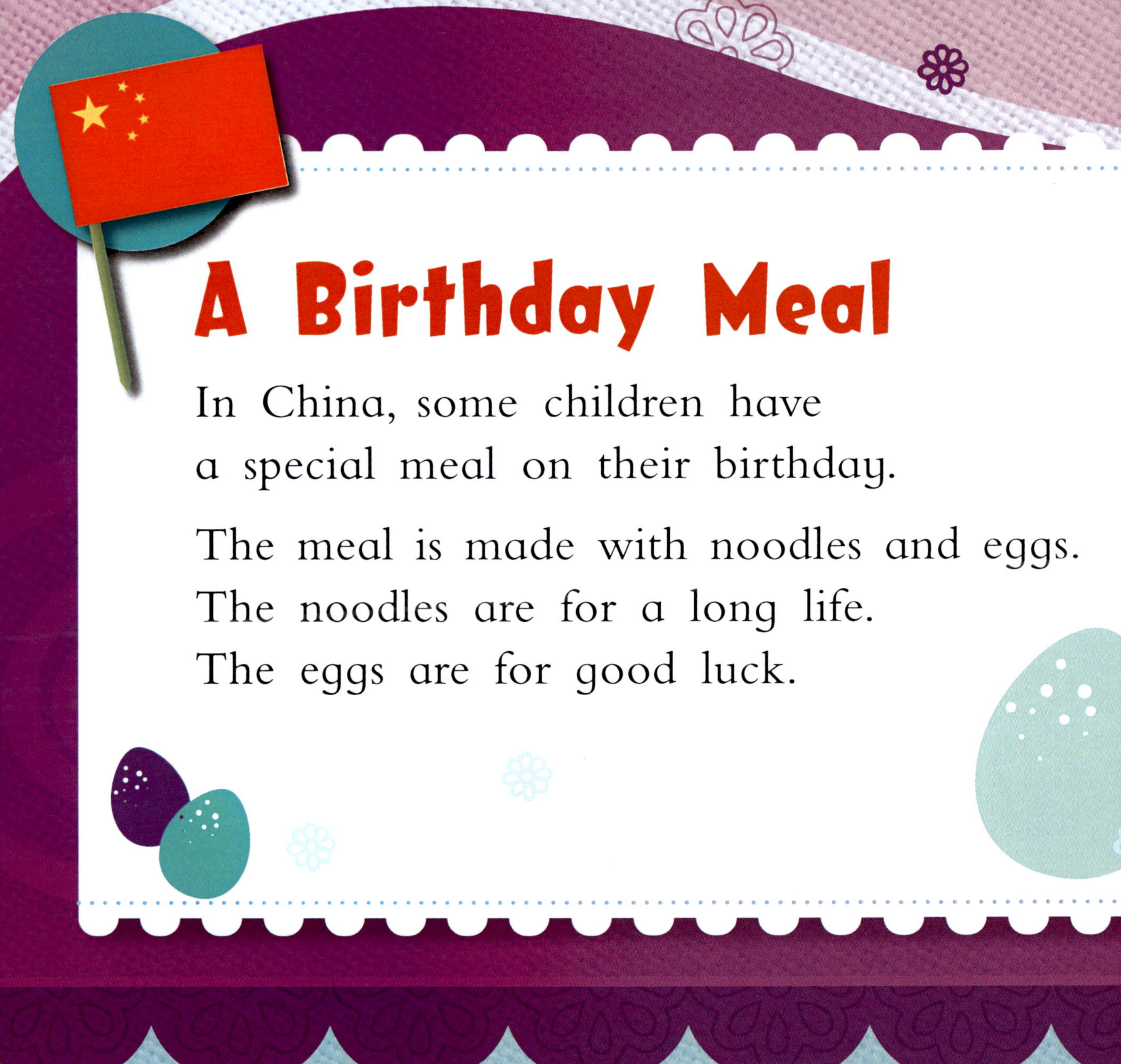

A Birthday Meal

In China, some children have a special meal on their birthday.

The meal is made with noodles and eggs. The noodles are for a long life. The eggs are for good luck.

A Birthday Surprise

In Mexico, some children have a **piñata** (say *pin-yaa-ta*) at their birthday party.

Children hit the piñata with a stick. The piñata breaks and toys or lollies fall out.

Glossary

celebrate to have fun at a special time, such as a birthday

hibiscus a bright flower that grows in warm, wet regions of the world

parcel something wrapped up; a package

piñata a decorated object filled with lollies and toys that is broken open at a party

wreath a ring or circle that is decorated